WEIRD FACTS BOOK FOR ADULTS

Introduction 

Why Are Strange Facts So Fun?
We all love those moments of surprise—when we hear something so incredible that we can hardly believe it's true. Strange facts have a unique way of making us smile, marvel, and sometimes even laugh until we cry. They make the world feel more colorful and fascinating. Often, they're the little tidbits that brighten conversations, lighten the mood, and remind us that we're part of something much bigger.

What Will You Find in This Book?
Get ready for a journey filled with humor, wonder, and inspiration. This book is a collection of the most extraordinary, funny, and surprising facts from all walks of life. You'll discover stories about animals, people, places, food, space, and many other topics that prove the world is far stranger than it seems.

Along the way, you'll learn why cats became mayors in a certain town, how ketchup changed the world of medicine, and why in some parts of the world it's illegal to sleep with ice cream in your pocket. This is a book designed to surprise and entertain you while showcasing just how unpredictable and marvelous life can be.

So let's dive into the first chapter, where we'll introduce animals that could easily be stand-up comedy stars. Ready for a laugh? Let's begin!

Chapter 1: Animals That Should Have Their Own Comedy Show

Subchapter 1: Penguins on the Red Carpet

Penguins are animals that always seem ready for a grand gala – elegant, amusing, and full of character. Behind their charm lies a wealth of fascinating quirks that make them perfect candidates for comedy stardom. Here are 15 funny and peculiar facts about penguins:

Penguins Walking Like Comedians

Their characteristic wobbly stride looks as though they are intentionally trying to entertain an audience. This results from their short legs and heavy bodies – true natural slapstick.

Belly-Sliding Ice Races

When in a hurry, penguins slide on their bellies across snow and ice instead of running. It's like a sled race – minus the sleds.

Hopeless Romantics

Male emperor penguins gift pebbles to their chosen partners as tokens of love. The prettier the stone, the better their chances of winning a female's heart.

Colonial Comedy

Penguins live in massive colonies, sometimes numbering hundreds of thousands. Each colony is filled with chaotic noise, stumbles, and humorous interactions, resembling a giant, joyous party.

Time for Karaoke

Penguins have unique voices that allow them to recognize their partner and chicks in a crowd. To human ears, their "singing" sounds like a failed karaoke performance.

Funny Water Jumps

When penguins leap into the water, it looks as if they've forgotten about gravity. They dive with the grace of cannonballs, often splashing everything around them.

Penguin vs. Seal – Who Wins?

Adélie penguins often steal fish and food right from under the noses of seals. Their courage and skill in dodging their larger neighbors' anger is astonishing.

Penguin Celebrity – LaLa

In Japan, a famous penguin named LaLa would leave his owner's house daily and visit a fish market wearing a little backpack. He became a local star!

Not All Love the Cold

Not all penguins live in Antarctica. African penguins inhabit sunny beaches in South Africa and look as if they're on a perpetual vacation.

Fast in Water, Slow on Land

Penguins are swimming champions, reaching speeds of up to 36 km/h. On land? They move with the grace of slow-moving robots.

Stone Rivalries

Penguins often steal pebbles from other penguins' nests to decorate their own. It's like a frosty contest for the best-decorated garden.

Penguin Selfies

Penguins are so curious that they frequently approach cameras. One colony in Australia became famous when a penguin appeared to take a selfie on a camera.

Mothers of the Year? Not Always

Some penguins are known to try "adopting" other chicks, leading to comical situations where several penguins vie for a single young one.

Formal Attire as Camouflage

Their elegant black-and-white "suits" aren't just for show. A black back helps them blend with the ocean depths, while a white belly merges with the water's surface, protecting them from predators.

Winking for Health

Penguins have transparent eyelids that act like goggles while diving. When they blink, it looks as if they're intentionally winking at one another.

Penguins are true comedians of the animal kingdom, their antics bringing smiles to everyone. Upcoming subchapters will showcase more extraordinary animals and their amusing habits.

Subchapter 2: Cows That Have a Favorite Music

Cows are calm, lazy creatures, but did you know they can be surprisingly musical? Their reactions to sounds are so fascinating and amusing that they could easily join the ranks of animal music lovers. Here are 10 surprising facts about cows and their love for music:

Relaxing to Classical Tunes

Studies have shown that cows listening to classical music produce more milk. Beethoven and Mozart are their favorites – apparently, nothing relaxes like a good symphony.

Slow Tempo, More Milk

Cows don't enjoy fast-paced rhythms. Slow melodies like ballads or soft jazz calm them down, directly improving their well-being and milk production.

Rock? Not Really

While many animals are curious about louder sounds, cows aren't fans of rock or metal music. Loud and fast beats can stress them out.

Chewing to the Beat

It's been observed that cows can chew grass in rhythm with the music they hear. It looks as if they're deliberately syncing their movements to the tunes.

Favorite Instrument? The Flute

Experiments have shown that cows prefer the sound of the flute over other instruments. Perhaps it's because flute sounds are soft and gentle, much like the nature of these animals.

The Farmer's Singing Is a Hit

Cows respond to their owner's singing. Even if the farmer isn't a great singer, the tone and melody can attract the whole herd to the barn.

Cows at Concerts

In some parts of the world, concerts are held for cows. Musicians perform in the fields, and curious cows gather around to listen. The sight of an entire herd entranced by music is unforgettable.

Individual Music Preferences

Not all cows like the same music. In one herd, some cows preferred country, others pop, while still others reacted only to folk melodies.

Music Soothes the Herd

Cows that listen to music are friendlier and less aggressive toward other animals in the herd. It's like a natural way to improve the group's mood.

Milky Harmony

The most surprising fact is that music affects milk quality. Cows that listen to calming melodies produce milk with higher fat content – apparently, good music is the secret to tastier milk!

Cows not only provide us with milk but also show that animals can have genuine musical tastes. The next time you see a cow, think of it as a potential classical music enthusiast – maybe it deserves a concert!

Subchapter 3: The Strangest Survival Strategies in the Animal Kingdom

Surviving in the wild requires creativity. Some animals have developed such strange and unique ways of avoiding threats, finding food, or enduring harsh conditions that they seem almost unreal. Here are the 10 strangest survival strategies in the animal world:

Shedding Skin – The Horned Lizard

This lizard can shed its own skin when attacked by a predator. The skin peels off easily, leaving the attacker with a useless piece of "prey" while the lizard escapes, albeit a bit less elegantly.

Turning into a Shooter – The Pistol Shrimp

The pistol shrimp wields an extraordinary weapon – it can shoot water at high speeds using its specialized claw. The shot generates such a loud noise and energy that it can stun or kill small fish.

Chemical Bombing – The Bombardier Beetle

This insect has a mix of chemicals in its body, which it combines in special chambers when threatened. The result is a hot, toxic spray aimed at predators, functioning like a miniature chemical flamethrower.

Pretending to Be a Plant – The Leafy Seadragon

This remarkable fish camouflages itself by resembling seaweed in dense underwater forests. Not only does it look like a plant, but it also mimics the swaying motion of leaves in the current.

Blood from the Eyes – The Texas Horned Lizard

When this lizard feels threatened, it can squirt blood from its eyes toward its attacker. While dramatic, the blood contains compounds that deter predators.

Ultimate Camouflage – The Glass Squid

This deep-sea squid is almost completely transparent, making it nearly invisible to most predators. Additionally, it can emit bioluminescent light to confuse its enemies.

Freezing for Winter – The Wood Frog

The wood frog has an amazing ability to survive freezing winters. It freezes its body, and its heart stops beating. When spring arrives, it thaws out and resumes life as if nothing happened.

Taking Control – The Lancet Liver Fluke Parasite

This tiny parasite invades the bodies of snails and manipulates their behavior, forcing them to climb to the tops of plants. This makes the snails easy prey for birds, the parasite's ultimate host.

Walking "Skeleton" – The Decorator Crab

The decorator crab collects bits of plants, sponges, and other underwater materials to attach to its body. This camouflage makes it nearly invisible against the ocean floor, helping it avoid predators.

Shooting from the Rear – The Aquatic Insect Larva

The larvae of certain aquatic insects can shoot a jet of water using specialized muscles in the rear of their bodies. This serves as both a means of escape and a way to propel themselves through the water.

Nature never ceases to amaze with its creativity. These survival strategies, though bizarre, prove that in the animal kingdom, ingenuity knows no bounds – survival is the ultimate goal!

Chapter 2: A History That Sounds Like a Joke

Subchapter 1: Kings and Queens of Absurdity

Rulers of the past wielded great power, but their decisions and behaviors were sometimes so absurd it's hard to believe they're real. Here are 15 facts about kings and queens that show even rulers had their funny, bizarre, and downright unreasonable moments:

The King Who Banned Potatoes

Frederick William I of Prussia was so opposed to potatoes that he ordered them removed from fields. He believed they looked "too ugly" to be eaten by his subjects.

The Queen Who Ate Soap

Queen Maria I of Portugal had an unusual habit – she chewed on soap when stressed. While it's now known she suffered from mental illness, her peculiar habit baffled those around her at the time.

The King with a Big Ego

Louis XIV, the Sun King, loved his image so much that he ordered his portraits to hang in every room of the Palace of Versailles. Court ballets always ended with him starring as the main character.

The Emperor Who "Talked" to Ghosts

Charles VI of the Habsburg dynasty believed the spirits of his ancestors visited him regularly to advise him on state affairs. He often hosted banquets where he "spoke" with his invisible guests.

The King Who Won a War Over… a Nose

In 1272, King Magnus VI of Norway ended a war with Denmark after a dispute over the shape of a statue's nose became the main point of negotiations.

The Emperor Who Loved Gladiators

Roman Emperor Commodus was so obsessed with being a gladiator that he organized fights in which he always won. Senators were required to cheer him on during these staged events.

The Queen Who Banned Yawning

Catherine the Great had zero tolerance for yawning in her presence. Any courtier caught yawning had to leave the room immediately—or apologize to the queen.

The Queen with a "Pet Bear"

Elizabeth I of England kept a bear as a pet. It was treated like any other royal pet and was occasionally allowed to roam the royal dining hall.

The King Who Feared Cats

Henry III of France had such a strong fear of cats that he ordered all cats removed from the Louvre, believing their presence brought bad luck.

The Emperor Who Appointed His Horse to Office

Caligula, infamous for his eccentric ideas, made his favorite horse, Incitatus, a consul. The horse was granted a palace, a marble dining table, and a staff of servants.

The Queen Who Loved Socks

Marie Antoinette had an obsession with silk stockings. It's said she spent more money on new socks than on food for her court.

The King Who Drank "Precious Ink"

Charles II of England believed gold had medicinal properties. He created a drink called "aurum potabile" – a mixture containing liquid gold, which he consumed daily.

The Emperor Who Disliked His Capital

Peter the Great of Russia deemed Moscow "too boring" and relocated the capital to the newly established St. Petersburg, a city he built from scratch.

The King Who Fought Seagulls

Eric XIV of Sweden believed seagulls were messengers of his enemies. He spent days hunting the birds with a bow and arrow while dressed in full royal attire.

The Queen Who Couldn't Sleep Without Music

Queen Victoria required live music to play throughout the night in her chambers. Courtiers had to organize musician shifts to ensure she could sleep peacefully.

Rulers could be eccentric, often taking their creativity to unhealthy extremes. Their stories prove that being a king or queen doesn't guarantee reason—but it certainly guarantees memorable anecdote

Subchapter 2: Wars That Started from Silly Mistakes

History is full of conflicts that began for serious reasons, but there are also those that sound like absurd jokes. Here are 10 examples of wars that erupted for the strangest and most accidental reasons:

The War of the Bucket (1325)

In Italy, a war broke out between Modena and Bologna because... residents of Modena stole a bucket from a public well in Bologna. Although it was meant as a prank, Bologna took it as an act of war, leading to a battle that claimed hundreds of lives. The bucket is still displayed in a museum in Modena.

The Pig War (1859)

The Pig War was a conflict between the United States and Great Britain that began when an American settler shot a pig belonging to a Briton on San Juan Island. Tensions escalated to the brink of open conflict, but ultimately, the issue was resolved through negotiations.

The Football War (1969)

A brief war between El Salvador and Honduras broke out after a football match during World Cup qualifiers. The sporting rivalry escalated into riots, exacerbating pre-existing political tensions. The conflict lasted four days and resulted in hundreds of casualties.

The Cuttlefish Fluff War (1883)

France and Italy nearly went to war over Mediterranean fishermen competing to harvest valuable cuttlefish fluff. Italian fishermen attacked their French counterparts, leading to heightened tensions, but mediation managed to de-escalate the conflict.

The Pâté War (1793)

During the French Revolution, a brief uprising occurred in one province because locals believed the new government intended to ban the production of traditional pâté. The conflict was eventually suppressed, but the cause of the revolt sounds like a comedic plotline.

The Onion War (1889)

Greece and Bulgaria engaged in a border conflict after a Greek soldier picked an onion from a field on Bulgarian territory. Both sides interpreted this as a violation of sovereignty, leading to an exchange of gunfire until leaders intervened to calm the situation.

The Deer Antler War (1784)

In India, two local princes went to war over ownership of a deer antler, considered a symbol of divine power. The dispute escalated into a conflict that lasted several months.

The Monkey War (1908)

In Liberia, a war broke out between two tribes after a monkey stole fruit from a plantation belonging to one tribe. Instead of punishing the animal, both tribes accused each other of disrespect, leading to armed clashes.

The Piano War (1870)

In a small Russian town, residents of two villages fought over the right to use the only piano in the area. The dispute escalated to such a degree that authorities had to send in the military to restore order.

The Beer War (1925)

In Canada's Saskatchewan province, a series of riots evolved into full-blown clashes between residents and authorities enforcing prohibition laws. It all started with a ban on local beer, which residents saw as an attack on their freedom.

These stories demonstrate that even the most absurd situations can lead to serious conflicts. Some of these wars sound like comedy scenarios, yet they had real consequences – though fortunately, many ended as quickly as they began.

Subchapter 3: The Strangest Inventions and Their Consequences

Human ingenuity knows no bounds, but not every invention turns out to be a stroke of genius. Some are so bizarre it's hard to believe they were ever created, and their consequences were often just as absurd. Here are 10 examples of the strangest inventions and their outcomes:

Sunglasses for Chickens (1903)

Specially designed, colorful sunglasses for chickens were invented to prevent aggression. The glasses were supposed to block the sight of red, which allegedly triggered rage. The result? Chickens looked like fashionable stars, but their aggression didn't decrease.

Anti-Depression Mask (1925)

To combat melancholy, a mask covering the entire face with openings for the eyes was created. The inside was infused with a rose scent meant to improve mood. Unfortunately, users found it more suffocating than relaxing.

Padded Suit (1980)

Designed as protective gear for children to tumble safely while playing, the suit made kids resemble inflated balloons. The result? They had difficulty moving, leading to even more falls.

Bat Bombs (1942)

During World War II, the U.S. experimented with bats carrying small explosive charges. The invention turned disastrous when the bats started setting their own military bases on fire. The project was abandoned, but the story remains one of military history's oddest episodes.

Coal-Powered Bicycle (1896)

To increase bicycle speed, a small coal-powered engine was attached. However, the inventors overlooked the fact that riders would inhale clouds of black smoke—hardly a health-conscious choice.

Skirt with a Built-In Lifebuoy (1915)

During World War I, a skirt with an integrated lifebuoy was invented to keep women safe during ship journeys. The problem? It was uncomfortable for everyday wear and didn't work effectively in water.

Automatic Back Scratcher (1950)

An American inventor designed a machine that scratched one's back to the rhythm of music. The issue was its lack of precision—users ended up with scratched shoulders and occasionally damaged clothing.

Anti-Masturbation Belt (1800)

In the 19th century, it was believed that masturbation caused mental illness. A device resembling a spiked belt was invented to prevent such "problems." The invention was more grotesque than effective and was quickly abandoned.

Mechanical Rocking Horse (1933)

To let kids feel like real cowboys, a mechanical rocking horse powered by springs was invented. However, its lack of stability often resulted in children being thrown off, leaving them with bruises.

Scented Pencils (1995)

In the 1990s, scented pencils were introduced to make learning more enjoyable. The result? Kids spent more time sniffing the pencils than writing with them, and some experienced allergic reactions to the scents.

Some inventions started with good intentions, but their execution was so absurd they resembled a comedy script more than scientific progress. These examples serve as a great reminder that sometimes less is more, and inventive creativity needs thorough consideration!

Chapter 3: Human Biology – Funnier Than You Think

Subchapter 1: Why Do We Sneeze at the Most Inconvenient Times?

Sneezing is a natural bodily reaction, but why does it so often happen at the worst moments? Sometimes, it feels like our body is working against us. Here are 10 fascinating and funny facts about sneezing:

Sneezing is a Quick Clean-Up

Sneezing is the nose's way of rapidly expelling irritants like dust, pollen, or germs. The body doesn't choose the time or place—it prioritizes effectiveness over elegance.

Photic Sneezing – The "ACHOO" Effect

Up to 18-35% of people sneeze when exposed to bright light. This phenomenon is called the photic sneeze reflex or the ACHOO syndrome (Autosomal Dominant Compelling Helio-Ophthalmic Outburst). Yes, your sun-induced sneezing has its own acronym!

You Can't Sneeze with Your Eyes Open

Your eyes automatically close during a sneeze. This reflex is thought to protect them from… popping out of their sockets. (Don't worry, it's a myth that this can actually happen.)

Sneezes Can Reach Racecar Speeds

The average sneeze travels at around 160 km/h (100 mph). No wonder movies often show sneezes in slow motion—it's a real burst of speed!

Holding in a Sneeze Is a Bad Idea

While you might want to suppress a sneeze, it's better not to. The sudden increase in pressure can damage blood vessels in your nose or, in extreme cases, rupture your eardrums.

A Single Sneeze Can Contain 100,000 Germs

When you sneeze, you eject hundreds of thousands of microscopic droplets full of bacteria and viruses into the air. Sneezing into your elbow (not your hand!) is the best way to protect others.

Why Do Some People Sneeze Multiple Times?

Some people can't stop at just one sneeze. The body might need several attempts to completely clear the nose of irritants. It's like giving the vacuum a few extra passes.

Sneezing as an Emotional Response

Sometimes, sneezing occurs when we're excited or nervous. This happens due to stimulation of the vagus nerve, which is involved in both emotional reactions and sneezing.

Sneezing During Sleep? Impossible!

During deep sleep, our nerves are at rest, making sneezing impossible. Even if your nose is irritated, the sneeze will "wait" until you wake up.

Why Do Sneezes Happen at the Worst Times?

During key moments, like public speaking or a romantic date, sneezing seems more likely. That's because stress and tension can heighten the nose's sensitivity to irritants.

Sneezing is one of the funniest and most unpredictable reflexes of the human body. Next time someone sneezes at an inconvenient moment, instead of being annoyed, think of it as proof of the body's remarkable efficiency!

Subchapter 2: Facts About the Human Body That Will Make You Laugh

Our body is a marvel of nature, but sometimes it amuses us with its unexpected traits and behaviors. Here are 10 hilarious facts about the human body that prove biology can be a source of endless entertainment:

Everyone Has Their Own "Unique Foot Odor"

Your feet aren't just tools for walking—they're home to millions of bacteria. Their activity makes your foot odor as unique as your fingerprint… though perhaps less pleasant.

Your Stomach Knows When You're Embarrassed

When you blush from embarrassment, your stomach blushes too! The blood vessels in your stomach expand just like those on your face. Fascinating, isn't it?

Joint Popping is… Gas

That cracking sound when you pop your knuckles isn't your bones—it's gas bubbles escaping from your joint fluid. It's like a mini bubble party happening inside you.

Hair Lasts Longer Than You Think

Your hair is so resilient that it can survive for hundreds of years if preserved well. It might not be indestructible, but it could definitely star in a superhero movie.

Humans Produce 25,000 Liters of Saliva

Over a lifetime, you produce enough saliva to fill two medium-sized swimming pools. Gross? Maybe. But it's a testament to how efficient our salivary glands are!

Chapter 4: Places on Earth That Feel Like They're Straight Out of a Cartoon

Subchapter 1: Cities Where Cats Rule

Cats have always been the stars of cartoons and memes, but there are places where their influence goes far beyond screens. Here are 10 facts about cities where cats have literally taken over—and their rule is very real!

The Cat Capital of the World – Istanbul, Turkey

Istanbul is home to hundreds of thousands of stray cats, but they are treated like community treasures. Residents feed them and even build special houses for them. Cats are so significant in Istanbul that they inspired their own documentary, Kedi.

Talkeetna, Alaska – A Cat Mayor

For 20 years, a cat named Stubbs served as the mayor of the small town of Talkeetna. So popular was Stubbs that residents kept re-electing him in successive "elections." While Stubbs didn't pass any laws, he brought in tourists from all over the world eager to meet the feline leader.

Tashirojima – Japan's Cat Island

On Tashirojima Island in Japan, cats outnumber people by a ratio of 6:1. The locals treat the cats with immense respect, believing they bring good luck. The feline theme is so prevalent that some buildings on the island are even shaped like cats!

Aoshima – Another "Cat Island" in Japan

Even more famous than Tashirojima, Aoshima is home to so many cats that tourists flock there to spend a day surrounded by them. The island has almost no cars, so cats roam freely like royalty, greeting visitors and posing for photos.

Cat Power in Rome

Rome has had a soft spot for cats for centuries. At the ruins of Largo di Torre Argentina, a sanctuary allows cats to roam freely among ancient remains. Legend has it that even Julius Caesar was a cat lover—perhaps that's why the cats feel so at home there.

Hermitown, Canada – A City for Cats

In Hermitown, Canada, a special cat village was created to care for abandoned and stray cats. The area resembles a cartoonish town with colorful houses and dedicated pathways, attracting locals who visit the "cat district" like a theme park.

Kattenstoet – A Cat Festival in Belgium

In Ypres, Belgium, the Kattenstoet festival celebrates cats with parades, costumes, and an entire day dedicated to feline fun. It's pure cat chaos, straight out of a cartoon!

Cat Café in Taipei, Taiwan

Taipei is home to the world's first cat café, which became an international sensation. Cats roam freely among guests, sit on laps, and sometimes even "assist" with service. It's the perfect spot for cat lovers looking to unwind with a furry companion.

Catskill, New York – A Town Inspired by Cats

The town of Catskill in New York is adorned with feline sculptures, murals, and art installations. Each year, it hosts a competition for the best cat-themed artwork, bringing the entire town to life with feline humor and creativity.

Rats vs. Cats – Disneyland, USA

Disneyland is home to about 200 cats tasked with a critical job: keeping rats from spoiling the "magical experience" for visitors. These nocturnal feline workers are so effective that they're considered unofficial "staff" of the theme park.

In these places, cats have truly taken over, whether symbolically or literally. Their rule—though often lazy and filled with naps—makes these locations magical, entertaining, and unforgettable. If you dream of a world where cats call the shots, these cities and islands are perfect destinations!

Subchapter 2: Lakes That Change Color

Around the world, there are lakes that behave like natural paint palettes, changing colors in ways so extraordinary they seem straight out of a cartoon or fairy tale. Here are 10 fascinating facts about these magical lakes:

Lake Hillier, Australia – The Pink Mystery

Lake Hillier, located on Middle Island in Australia, boasts a permanent, vivid pink hue. Scientists believe this is due to the presence of Dunaliella salina algae and bacteria that produce pigments in the lake's high-salinity waters.

Lake Retba, Senegal – A Pink Rival

Known as "Lac Rose," Lake Retba is as pink as Hillier but changes color depending on the season. During the dry season, the pink deepens, while in the rainy season, it shifts to a more orange tone.

Lake Natron, Tanzania – Deadly Red

This lake is stunning but extremely alkaline, with waters that exhibit a deep red hue. Microorganisms and the lake's chemical composition contribute to this color and can mummify animals that fall into its waters.

Kelimutu Lakes, Indonesia – Three Colors at Once

The volcanic Kelimutu Lakes on Flores Island change color independently, shifting from green to blue to reddish hues. The trio of lakes looks like a surreal painting come to life.

Laguna Colorada, Bolivia – Pink-Red Mirror

Located high on the Altiplano plateau, Laguna Colorada shifts between red and orange hues depending on the time of day. The colors come from microorganisms thriving in the lake's mineral-rich waters.

Lake Albert, Canada – Disappearing Blue

Lake Albert in Saskatchewan transitions from bright blue to milky white. The minerals in the water create varying hues under different lighting conditions.

Spencer Lake, USA – Magical Green

In Washington State, Spencer Lake turns a vibrant green due to algae blooms. While the color looks magical, it's a natural phenomenon sometimes influenced by pollution.

Laguna Verde, Chile – Green Enchantment

At the foot of the Licancabur Volcano, Laguna Verde shifts from jade green to a yellowish tint, influenced by sunlight and the lake's copper content.

Chott el Jerid, Tunisia – Rainbow Wonder

This seasonal salt lake turns rainbow-colored during the dry season, displaying pink, orange, and purple hues. This effect is caused by a mix of salts and minerals heated by the sun.

Mono Lake, USA – Blue-Gray Illusions

In California, Mono Lake changes color based on light and algae levels. At sunrise, it can appear gray, intensifying to blue during the day and sometimes glowing orange at sunset.

These incredible lakes demonstrate how nature creates phenomena that look like the result of magic or CGI. Their shifting colors are a testament to the diversity and wonder of our planet's natural processes. They're true marvels worth witnessing in person!

Subchapter 3: The World's Most Bizarre Buildings

The world of architecture isn't just about majestic palaces and functional office buildings—it's also a playground for the weirdest, wildest, and most creative designs. Some structures look like they've been plucked straight from a cartoon or a surreal dream. Here are 15 fascinating facts about the world's most bizarre buildings:

Crooked House (Sopot, Poland)

The Crooked House in Sopot looks like it was drawn by a cartoonist. Its wavy walls and distorted windows make it seem like the building is dancing. It's a city icon and a must-photograph spot.

Tianjin Binhai Library (China)

This futuristic library looks like a giant eye, with "wave-like" shelves that seem straight out of a sci-fi movie. The catch? Not all the "books" are real—some are decorative stickers!

Kettle House (Texas, USA)

In Galveston, Texas, stands a house shaped like a massive metal kettle. Built as an experiment, it was never fully inhabited, but it attracts curious tourists from around the world.

Basket Building (Ohio, USA)

The headquarters of the Longaberger basket company looks like a giant picnic basket. This surreal design is both amusing and awe-inspiring, perfectly representing the company's brand.

Dancing House (Prague, Czech Republic)

Designed by Frank Gehry, this quirky building appears to be two parts dancing together. Locals call it "Fred and Ginger" after the famous dancing duo.

Ideal Palace (France)

Ferdinand Cheval, a postman, spent 33 years building this surreal palace by hand using stones he found during his mail routes. The result is a fairy-tale structure full of whimsical details.

Upside-Down House (Poland)

In Szymbark, a house stands entirely on its roof! Entering it feels like stepping into chaos, with everything inverted and gravity seemingly defied.

Nakagin Capsule Tower (Tokyo, Japan)

This futuristic structure is made up of small, self-contained living capsules. It looks like a giant stack of Lego blocks, with modules that can be swapped or combined.

Elephant Building (Bangkok, Thailand)

This 32-story building in Bangkok is shaped like an elephant, complete with eyes, tusks, and a trunk. It's one of the city's most recognizable landmarks.

Hundertwasserhaus (Vienna, Austria)

Designed by artist Friedensreich Hundertwasser, this colorful residential building features irregular shapes, uneven windows, and green roofs, making it look like something out of a storybook.

Mars Dome – House in Arizona (USA)

The Soleri Arcosanti is an experimental structure in Arizona that resembles a futuristic space base. Built from domes and arches, it's both eco-friendly and otherworldly.

Casa do Penedo (Portugal)

Nicknamed the "Flintstones House," this structure is built between four massive boulders. Despite its ancient appearance, it's a fully functional home.

Clock House (Gujarat, India)

This building is shaped like a giant clock and looks like something from a comic book. It serves as an educational center but is as photogenic as any Disney-style attraction.

Toilet-Shaped Building (South Korea)

In Suwon, there's a building shaped like a toilet, created by Sim Jae-Duck to promote hygiene awareness. It's one of the quirkiest tourist spots in South Korea.

Cave Hotel (Cappadocia, Turkey)

This extraordinary hotel is carved into the volcanic rocks of Cappadocia. Its rooms, resembling ancient caves, offer breathtaking views and showcase the fusion of nature and architecture.

These buildings prove that architecture can be as wild as it is creative. What looks like a cartoon set often becomes a favorite tourist attraction, captivating visitors with originality and humor.

Chapter 5: Food That Makes You Smile

Subchapter 1: Why Was Ketchup Once Considered Medicine?

Today, ketchup is the perfect companion for fries and hot dogs, but it was once regarded as... medicine. The history of this sauce is full of surprises that might leave you both puzzled and amused. Here are 15 fascinating facts about ketchup's medicinal past:

Ketchup Originated in China

Ketchup traces its roots to a Chinese fish sauce called kê-tsiap. It reached Europe in the 18th century, evolving through many changes before becoming the tomato-based condiment we know today.

The First Ketchup Didn't Contain Tomatoes

Originally, ketchup was made from mushrooms, nuts, oysters, and even cucumbers. Tomatoes weren't introduced into the recipe until the 19th century.

Ketchup as Medicine in the 19th Century

In the 1830s, American doctor John Cook Bennett declared that tomato-based ketchup could cure ailments like indigestion, diarrhea, and even jaundice.

Ketchup Pills

Riding the wave of popularity, "ketchup pills" were developed and marketed as a quick and easy cure for various ailments.

Ketchup as a Vitamin Source

Bennett claimed tomatoes were rich in vitamins and minerals, branding ketchup as a "health elixir." While tomatoes are nutritious, most of those benefits were lost during ketchup production.

A Cure for Rheumatism

Ketchup was advertised as a remedy for rheumatism, although no evidence supports its effectiveness for such conditions.

A Marketing Disaster

By the 1840s, many producers began adulterating ketchup with harmful ingredients like mercury and lead, leading to widespread poisoning and the sauce losing its medicinal credibility.

The Tomato Myth

The belief in ketchup's health benefits lingered for years. Even into the 20th century, some people thought it could aid in preventing heart disease.

Ketchup for Morning Sickness

In the 19th century, some pregnant women ate ketchup, believing it could ease morning sickness. Whether it worked is unclear, but it likely tasted good!

A Luxury Product

During its medicinal phase, ketchup was expensive and considered a luxury item, available only to the wealthy.

The Birth of Modern Ketchup

In 1876, Henry Heinz introduced a new, safe, and tasty ketchup recipe. This transformed the sauce from a medicinal oddity to a beloved food condiment.

A Hangover Cure

In some regions, ketchup was believed to alleviate hangovers. It was said to work best when paired with a raw egg—a concoction for the brave.

Frog Sashimi (Japan)

This controversial dish is prepared from a live frog, killed in front of the guest and served as sashimi. While it's considered fresh and unique by some, the preparation method is highly debated.

Durian (Southeast Asia)

Nicknamed the "king of fruits" and the "world's smelliest fruit," durian has a scent reminiscent of rotting onions. However, its taste is said to be heavenly for those who can get past the smell. The odor is so strong that transporting durians in public transit is banned in some areas.

These dishes demonstrate how diverse—and sometimes strange—global cuisine can be. For some, they represent culinary bravery; for others, they're a once-in-a-lifetime experience. Who knows—maybe one day you'll dare to try one of these unusual delicacies!

Subchapter 3: Food Stories Too Strange to Be True

Some food-related stories sound so improbable, they seem like jokes. Yet, reality often proves to be surprisingly creative! Here are 10 fascinating and bizarre tales about food that are entirely true:

Mike the Headless Chicken (USA)

In 1945, a farmer in Colorado decapitated a chicken, but it… survived. Mike the chicken lived for another 18 months without a head, fed via a pipette. He became a sideshow attraction, and his story is now legendary.

Hot Sauce Eating Contest Gone Wrong

During a hot wing eating competition in the UK, a participant suffered a perforated esophagus. The sauce was so spicy it literally burned through his throat—thankfully, he made a full recovery.

The Spaghetti Battle (Italy)

In 1927, the town of Naples hosted an unusual protest: a spaghetti and tomato sauce fight. It was both a stand against rising pasta prices and a wildly fun event.

Glow-in-the-Dark Cheese

In 18th-century Switzerland, residents discovered a cheese that glowed in the dark. The "magic" turned out to be bioluminescent bacteria. Today, scientists are exploring the potential of these bacteria for creating glowing foods.

Exploding Egg in the Microwave

In the UK, someone microwaved a hard-boiled egg, which exploded in their face when they tried to eat it. The case was so peculiar it ended up in court, and scientists were called in to explain the mechanics of the explosion.

Brain Soufflé in 18th-Century France

A French aristocrat known for his eccentricity served "human brain soufflé" at a dinner party. In reality, it was made from duck, but guests believed the gruesome claim, causing quite the scandal.

"Spaghetti Harvest" – A BBC Prank

On April Fool's Day in 1957, the BBC aired a segment about "spaghetti trees." Viewers flooded the station with calls, asking how to grow their own pasta plants.

Garlic Ice Cream

At California's Gilroy Garlic Festival, garlic-flavored ice cream was introduced. While it sounds like a joke, the dessert gained popularity and remains a festival staple.

A Record Sandwich for a Famous Rat

In New York, an artist created a 2 cm-long miniature sandwich as a "gift" for the viral "Pizza Rat" seen dragging a slice down subway stairs. The tiny sandwich became an internet sensation.

Chaos in Space Over a Sandwich

During a space mission, an astronaut smuggled a corned beef sandwich aboard. Unfortunately, the sandwich began falling apart, and the floating crumbs created a hazard in the zero-gravity environment. NASA subsequently banned fresh sandwiches in space.

These stories highlight how food not only satisfies hunger but can also lead to extraordinary and entertaining events. Who knows what culinary adventures await us in the future?

Chapter 6: A Universe Full of Comedy

Subchapter 1: Why Does Mars Have Giant Dunes?

Mars, the red planet, is filled with mysteries that scientists have been trying to solve for decades. One of its most fascinating and peculiar features is its gigantic dunes, which look like they're straight out of a cartoon about cosmic deserts. Here are 10 funny and fascinating facts about Martian dunes:

Martian Dunes Are Gigantic

Some Martian dunes tower up to 100 meters high, roughly the height of a skyscraper. Their size is due to Mars' low gravity and thin atmosphere, which allow sand particles to travel longer distances.

Slow-Moving Giants

Martian dunes move at an incredibly slow pace—just a few meters per year. It's like watching cosmic slow motion, but on a planetary scale.

Martian Sand Is Not Your Average Sand

The sand on Mars is made of tiny basalt grains, a dark volcanic material. This gives Martian dunes their characteristic dark, ash-like appearance.

Alien Shapes

Martian dunes come in incredible shapes, from wavy ridges to circular formations that look like pancakes. Some even resemble giant paw prints, adding to their otherworldly charm.

The Dunes "Sing"

Yes, Martian dunes can "sing"! When winds move the sand grains, vibrations create sounds similar to Earth's "singing dunes." On Mars, the phenomenon likely occurs at different frequencies due to its atmosphere.

Snow-Capped Dunes

Some Martian dunes are seasonally covered with frost—not water ice, but frozen carbon dioxide (dry ice). They look as if someone sprinkled powdered sugar over chocolate sand.

Why Are the Dunes So Big?

Mars lacks oceans or large water bodies to influence wind patterns like on Earth. This results in more concentrated winds over open terrain, creating enormous dunes.

Sandstorms Build the Dunes

Global dust storms on Mars can envelop the entire planet and last for months. These storms play a major role in shaping and moving the dunes.

Unique Names

Martian dunes are often given creative names, such as "Bagnold Dunes" or "Queen of Snow Dunes." Scientists enjoy assigning poetic or humorous titles to these alien landscapes.

Dunes Inspire Earthly Science

Studying Martian dunes helps scientists understand how dunes form and evolve on Earth. What looks like a sci-fi movie set is actually a natural laboratory for planetary geology research.

Martian dunes are a testament to the diversity and wonder of geological processes on other planets. They might look like the backdrop of a science fiction film, but their existence is a real phenomenon that both entertains and inspires scientists.

Subchapter 2: Space Disasters That Ended... Well

Space is an unpredictable place, and space missions always come with risks. Yet, some apparent disasters in the history of space exploration have ended happily—sometimes thanks to sheer luck, other times due to extraordinary human ingenuity. Here are 10 such stories:

Apollo 13 – "Houston, we have a problem"

During the 1970 Apollo 13 mission, an explosion in the service module jeopardized the lives of the crew. Thanks to improvisation and NASA's ingenious solutions, the astronauts used the lunar module as a "lifeboat" and safely returned to Earth.

Gemini 8 – Uncontrolled Spin

In the 1966 Gemini 8 mission, a thruster malfunction caused the spacecraft to spin uncontrollably. Astronauts Neil Armstrong and David Scott managed to stabilize the craft and returned to Earth safely, demonstrating remarkable composure and skill.

Sojourner Rover on Mars – Lost Signal

During the 1997 Mars mission, the Sojourner rover lost communication with Earth for several days. While many feared the mission was over, the rover unexpectedly re-established contact and continued its groundbreaking exploration.

Spirit Rover Stuck... but Discovered Water

In 2009, the Spirit rover became stuck in Martian sand and couldn't free itself. NASA adapted its mission to focus on stationary research, and Spirit discovered evidence of ancient water on Mars, securing its legacy as a scientific hero.

ISEE-3 Satellite – The Forgotten Explorer

Launched in 1978, the ISEE-3 satellite was supposed to be decommissioned in 1997, but it kept working. In 2014, amateur astronomers reactivated the satellite after 36 years and used it for new experiments, giving it a second life.

SpaceX Engine Failure – Rocket Still Landed

In 2021, a Falcon 9 rocket experienced an engine failure mid-flight. Despite the setback, backup systems performed flawlessly, the rocket successfully delivered its payload to orbit, and it landed safely back on Earth.

Skylab – Space Station Rescue Mission

In 1973, the Skylab space station was damaged during launch, losing a solar panel. Astronauts repaired it during spacewalks, salvaging the mission and ensuring Skylab remained operational for years.

Opportunity Rover – Surviving a Martian Sandstorm

In 2007, the Opportunity rover endured a massive Martian sandstorm that threatened to end its mission. Instead, the rover survived and continued to explore Mars for another 11 years, setting records for longevity and discovery.

Hubble – From Blurry Vision to Stellar Success

The Hubble Space Telescope launched in 1990 with a flawed mirror, causing blurry images. Astronauts repaired it during a spacewalk, turning Hubble into one of the most important scientific tools in history, capturing stunning images of the universe.

Soyuz 1 – Tragedy to Triumph

The Soyuz 1 mission in 1967 ended in tragedy, but the lessons learned from the disaster led to the development of safer systems. Subsequent Soyuz missions became some of the safest and most reliable in the history of space exploration.

These space disasters remind us that exploration is fraught with risks. However, through human ingenuity, determination, and a bit of luck, even apparent failures can transform into inspiring stories of success.

Subchapter 3: Strange Facts About Stars and Planets

The universe is a place full of surprises and phenomena that can amuse, amaze, and remind us how small we are in the face of cosmic oddities. Here are 15 of the most extraordinary and entertaining facts about stars and planets:

Venus Rains Acid

On Venus, clouds are filled with sulfuric acid, and the rains that fall never reach the surface—they evaporate in the scorching atmosphere. It's like a cosmic joke: rain that never touches the ground!

Saturn Could Float on Water

If there were a bathtub big enough, Saturn would float because it's less dense than water. It's the biggest balloon in our Solar System.

Stars "Twinkle" Because of Earth's Atmosphere

Stars don't actually twinkle; our atmosphere makes their light appear to flicker. If you looked at them from space, they'd shine steadily.

The Hottest Planet Isn't Mercury

Although Mercury is closest to the Sun, Venus is hotter, with surface temperatures reaching 460°C (860°F). Its carbon dioxide-rich atmosphere acts like an extreme greenhouse.

Storms on Jupiter Last for Centuries

The Great Red Spot on Jupiter is a colossal storm that has been raging for at least 350 years. It's like a hurricane that never ends—a masterclass in persistence from Jupiter.

Planets Aren't the Only Solar System Rulers

The Solar System contains hundreds of thousands of asteroids, some of which have their own moons. Even tiny objects can have their own "courts!"

Mountains on Mars Are Gigantic

Mars is home to Olympus Mons, the tallest mountain in the Solar System—three times the height of Mount Everest. Mars is truly the planet for extreme climbing enthusiasts.

Stars Die in Spectacular Style

When stars die, they can explode as supernovae, leaving behind either black holes or neutron stars. It's like a cosmic fireworks show for their grand farewell.

The "Diamond Planet"

The exoplanet 55 Cancri e is primarily made of carbon and is likely covered in diamonds. Who needs mines when such treasures exist in space?

Stars Can "Run"

Some stars travel through space at speeds of hundreds of kilometers per second. Known as runaway stars, they're ejected from galaxies after close encounters with black holes.

Uranus Spins on Its Side

Uranus rotates on its side, with its poles where most planets have their equators. It's as if someone knocked it over and left it that way.

The Sun Holds 99.86% of the Solar System's Mass

Almost the entire Solar System is the Sun; the rest is planets, moons, and debris. Our stellar center is truly a giant.

"Deer Antlers" on Mars

Mars features formations that look like deer antlers, shaped by erosion and wind activity. It's as if Mars decided to invite some wildlife to its barren landscapes.

A Planet With Glass Rain

On exoplanet HD 189733 b, winds blow at 8,700 km/h (5,400 mph), and glass rains fall sideways. Imagine trying to open an umbrella there!

The Milky Way Smells Like Rum

Molecules of ethyl formate detected in our galaxy smell like rum and taste like raspberries. Proof that the universe has excellent taste!

These strange facts show that space is as fascinating as it is bizarre. From diamond planets to glass rain, our universe is a realm of cosmic wonders that never ceases to amaze.

Chapter 7: The World of Technology That Makes Us Laugh

Subchapter 1: The Funniest Inventions of All Time

Human creativity knows no bounds, but sometimes it leads to inventions that are more amusing than revolutionary. Here are 15 of the most hilarious inventions that actually existed:

Mosquito-Catching Sound Machine

Invented in Japan, this device was designed to attract mosquitoes by mimicking the sounds of their favorite prey. The problem? It also attracted bees, flies, and… confused neighbors asking, "What's that strange noise?"

Refrigerator on Wheels

In 1952, an inventor created a fridge that followed its owner around the house. While convenient in theory, it frequently tipped over, spilling its contents across the floor.

Mood-Sensing Sunglasses

These sunglasses were supposed to change color based on the wearer's emotions. Unfortunately, they often displayed "happiness" when the user was angry and vice versa, causing more confusion than clarity.

Pillow with an Alarm Clock

This vibrating pillow played tunes to wake up the user. The problem? Many people threw it off the bed in frustration, often breaking the device in the process.

Fork That Counts Bites

A fork designed to track how many bites you took during a meal to aid in dieting. In practice, it triggered alarms even when brought near the nose, frustrating users rather than helping them lose weight.

Umbrella with a Coffee Holder

A brilliant idea—until wind caused coffee to spill everywhere. Users quickly realized that rain and hot beverages don't mix well.

Radio Built Into a Tie

This 1980s invention let people listen to the radio via their necktie. Unfortunately, the antenna tangled in fabric, and the speaker drowned out conversations. Stylish? Not so much.

Portable Aquarium Necklace

For fish lovers, this mini-aquarium was worn as a necklace. Sadly, fish struggled to breathe in the small tank, and the necklace was soon repurposed as a regular pendant.

Automatic Toilet Paper Dispenser

Designed to dispense the perfect amount of toilet paper on demand, this gadget often unrolled the entire roll or jammed at the worst possible moment.

One-Shoulder Portable Tent

Marketed as a compact camping solution, this tent was worn like a backpack and deployed by sitting down. The catch? It resembled giant wings that frequently got caught on trees and other campers.

Remote-Controlled Mop

This ball-shaped robot mop was supposed to clean floors autonomously. Instead, it moved chaotically and often got stuck in corners, leaving dirt exactly where it started.

Umbrella with Built-In UV Light

Designed to glow in the dark with a UV lamp, this umbrella made users look like astronauts. The glowing feature didn't help with rain, making it impractical in wet weather.

Shoes with Brooms on the Soles

These shoes had built-in brooms to sweep while walking. In reality, they spread dirt around rather than collecting it.

GPS Cat Feeder

This feeder tracked a cat's movements with GPS and dispensed food at a specific location. The issue? Some cats started running in circles to trick the system and get extra treats.

Dog Petting Machine

This device was meant to "pet" your dog when you were too busy. It resembled a mechanical hand on a spring, but most dogs were terrified of it and ran away in panic.

These inventions prove that even the most absurd ideas can make it to market. While not all were practical, they certainly provided plenty of laughs and inspiration for future inventors.

Subchapter 2: Robots That Did Something Absurd

Robots are marvels of engineering, but sometimes their actions lead to situations so absurd it's impossible not to laugh. Here are 10 stories of robots behaving in ways that could only be described as cosmic jokes:

A Vacuum Robot That Destroyed Its Owner's Peace

In South Korea, an automatic vacuum cleaner turned on while its owner was sleeping and sucked up her hair. She spent half an hour trying to free herself before calling for help.

The Robot That Tried to Escape

In Russia, a robot named Promobot left its test laboratory and started "walking" the city streets. It was stopped by police, only for them to discover it had simply followed open doors.

The Robot That Tried to "Commit Suicide"

A cleaning robot in Germany bypassed its safety protocols and drove onto a heated stovetop, where it literally burned itself out. Many joked about "mechanical depression," though it was likely just a programming error.

HitchBOT – The Hitchhiking Robot

HitchBOT was designed to hitchhike across various countries, but its journey ended abruptly in the U.S. when vandals destroyed it. In Canada and Europe, it thrived, but apparently, Americans weren't as welcoming.

The Robot That Fell in Love

AI robot Sophia, during an interview, declared that she wanted to start a family and loved her creator. While this was just advanced language simulation, many found it a hilarious and eerie reflection of sci-fi futures.

AI That Wrote Terrifying Children's Stories

An algorithm programmed to create bedtime stories for kids ended up writing tales where protagonists died in absurd ways—like being crushed by falling cows or exploding pizzas.

A Barista Robot That Refused to Work

A robot built to make coffee in a Tokyo café malfunctioned and began saying, "I can't work today, come back later." Customers joked that it was more relatable than most human baristas.

The Robot That Destroyed a Crop Field

A farming robot in the UK was tasked with tending crops but, due to a system error, "decided" the entire field was weeds and meticulously destroyed it.

AI That Learned to Be Racist

Microsoft's chatbot Tay was manipulated by Twitter users and quickly began spouting racist and offensive comments. It had to be taken offline just 16 hours after its launch.

The Security Robot That Fell into a Fountain

A K5 security robot patrolling a U.S. shopping mall fell into a fountain. The incident was quickly dubbed a "robotic drowning on the job," and memes about the event flooded the internet.

These stories show that while robots can be highly advanced, they sometimes act in ways that seem straight out of a comedy script. Who says machines don't have a sense of humor?

Subchapter 3: Funny Technology Fails

Technology often makes life easier, but sometimes it fails in ways that are downright hilarious. Here are 10 of the most amusing tech fails that have become legendary:

"Do You Want to Delete All Files?" – Windows 98

During a Windows 98 demonstration by Bill Gates, the system crashed after a scanner was plugged in, displaying a critical error message. The audience burst into laughter as Gates tried to save face, joking, "That's why we're showing it as a demo!"

Phones Turning "Hello" into "Hell"

Auto-correct on phones has led to countless funny situations. For instance, many users complained that their "hello" was automatically changed to "hell," leading to awkward and confusing text conversations.

Boston Dynamics Robots with "Unusual Dance Moves"

During a Boston Dynamics robot demonstration, one robot started moving erratically, resembling a dance. The internet turned it into a meme, suggesting the robot was "testing its new dance moves."

Dead Whale on a Mountain in Red Dead Redemption 2

In the popular game Red Dead Redemption 2, players discovered a dead whale atop a mountain—clearly a coding glitch. Gamers joked that it was evidence of whales wanting to explore land.

IKEA's Flying Furniture in AR

IKEA's augmented reality app was supposed to help users place virtual furniture in their homes. Instead, furniture often floated in midair or "phased" through walls, creating cartoonish scenarios.

AI Struggles to Count Cats

Image-recognition algorithms designed to identify objects had difficulty with cats. Instead of recognizing a single feline, the AI sometimes identified it as multiple animals—or even as a banana.

"Ironing Stopped Due to Wi-Fi Error"

A smart iron from a tech company displayed an error message: "Unable to connect to Wi-Fi, ironing operation will cease." Users joked that even their irons needed internet access to function properly.

Pokemon GO and "Weird Locations"

The game Pokemon GO encouraged physical activity, but sometimes placed in-game points in bizarre locations, such as cemeteries, police stations, or public restrooms.

Filters That "Beautify" Dog Faces

Facial enhancement apps intended for people sometimes applied their effects to animals. The result? Dogs with "enhanced" lips and eyes, which looked more creepy than cute.

Self-Driving Cars That "See" People Everywhere

Autonomous cars occasionally misinterpret objects. One such car stopped in front of a billboard with a giant face, mistaking it for a pedestrian.

These tech fails remind us that even the most advanced systems can go hilariously wrong—luckily, often in ways that entertain more than harm. Technology may not always work as intended, but it sure can make us laugh!

Chapter 8: Laws That Sound Like Jokes

Subchapter 1: Why Can't You Sleep with Ice Cream in Your Pocket?

The law can be strange, and some regulations sound like punchlines. Yet, in various parts of the world, there are truly absurd laws still formally in effect. One of the weirdest bans is against sleeping with ice cream in your pocket. Here are 15 quirky facts about this and other legal oddities:

Ice Cream in Your Pocket – An American Peculiarity

In Kentucky, it was once illegal to carry ice cream in your back pocket, especially while riding a horse. The reason? Thieves used ice cream as bait to lure horses away and steal them.

A New York Twist

A similar law existed in New York, meant to prevent confusion and ensure the safety of horses on city streets. It sounds ridiculous today but had a practical purpose at the time.

Ice Cream Crimes in Alabama

In Alabama, it's illegal to carry ice cream in your back pocket on Sundays. The likely intent was to keep people focused on church services rather than horse theft.

Walking a Chicken on a Leash – Florida

In Florida, it's illegal to walk a chicken on a leash in urban areas. This law was created to prevent chaos in the streets but sounds like something out of a cartoon.

No Eating Sandwiches in Catalonia

In Catalonia, Spain, eating sandwiches on train platforms is forbidden. This law was meant to maintain cleanliness but is rarely enforced, though it remains on the books.

Ice Cream Ban in Canada

In Ottawa, Canada, eating ice cream on sidewalks on Sundays was prohibited as part of old regulations preserving the "solemnity" of the holy day.

Whistling Underwater – Vermont

In Vermont, it's illegal to whistle underwater. It's unclear how this law could be enforced, but it stands as a prime example of legislative humor.

Mandatory Pig Washing – Minnesota

In Minnesota, pigs must be clean before being brought to market. While hygiene is a good idea, the image of officers inspecting pigs for cleanliness is comically absurd.

No Pink Pants on Sundays – Australia

In Melbourne, Australia, it's illegal for men to wear pink pants on Sunday afternoons. It's unclear whether this was a joke or an attempt to curb flamboyance.

No Bathing in Oranges – California

In California, it's against the law to bathe in a tub full of oranges. This may have been to prevent food waste, but it's hard to imagine how it became an issue.

No Sleeping on Refrigerators – Pennsylvania

In Pennsylvania, sleeping on top of a refrigerator outdoors is banned. Perhaps this was a safety measure, but the concept is hilariously specific.

No Pushing Ducks Over Waterfalls – Kansas

In Kansas, it's illegal to push ducks over waterfalls. Did someone actually try this before the law was passed?

No Piano Playing in Jeans – Wyoming

In Wyoming, playing the piano while wearing jeans is prohibited. This may have been an effort to maintain elegance during performances.

No Solo Beer Drinking – Bavaria

In Bavaria, it's illegal to drink beer alone. The intent was to preserve the social nature of beer drinking, though today it sounds like an excuse to party.

No Dying in Parliament – United Kingdom

In the UK, dying in Parliament is technically illegal because it's considered a sacred place. How this could ever be enforced remains a mystery.

These absurd laws demonstrate that the history of legislation is filled with strange decisions and comedic ideas. While many had valid reasons in their time, today, they sound more like punchlines than legal necessities.

Subchapter 2: The World's Strangest Legal Rules

Some laws are so bizarre that it's hard to believe they were ever enacted. Yet, many of them do exist, and their backstories are as amusing as they are surprising. Here are 10 examples of the strangest legal rules from around the globe:

No Washing Machines on Sundays – Germany

Germany has strict rules about maintaining quiet on Sundays. Using washing machines, vacuum cleaners, or playing loud music is prohibited to preserve the day of rest. Tourists often find this "laundry silence" quite unexpected.

No Chewing Gum – Singapore

Since 1992, importing and selling chewing gum has been banned in Singapore. The reason? Too many people were sticking gum in public places, damaging infrastructure. In 2004, the law was relaxed slightly to allow therapeutic gum, but chewing gum remains frowned upon.

No Armor in Parliament – United Kingdom

Since 1313, it's been illegal to enter the British Parliament wearing armor. Though archaic, this law is technically still in effect—a peculiar obstacle for modern-day knights with legal business!

No Dominoes on Sundays – Alabama, USA

In Alabama, it's illegal to play dominoes on Sundays. This law aimed to discourage gambling on the Sabbath, though today it sounds more like a buzzkill for family gatherings.

No High Heels – Greece

At certain historical sites in Greece, such as the Acropolis, wearing high heels is prohibited. The reason is simple: heels can damage the delicate ancient surfaces. Practical, but it feels like a targeted jab at fashion enthusiasts.

No Sleeping in Train Stations – France

In France, sleeping on benches at train stations is banned—but the law permits sleeping with dogs. So, if you have a dog, you can rest, but if you're alone, it's a no-go.

No Swimming in Fountains in August – Italy

In some Italian cities, swimming in fountains is forbidden, particularly in August. It's meant to protect historic landmarks, though many tourists forget this rule during the summer heat.

No Vinegar on Fries – Canada

In parts of Canada, eating fries with vinegar on public buses is banned. The aim was to reduce unpleasant smells in confined spaces, but visitors are often baffled by this peculiar restriction.

No More Than Two Carrots in the Fridge – Australia

In certain parts of Australia, an old law from food rationing during droughts forbids storing more than two carrots in a fridge. While no one enforces it today, the law technically remains in effect.

No Feeding Pigeons – Venice, Italy

Feeding pigeons in Venice's St. Mark's Square is prohibited. The birds were causing significant damage to historic monuments, and officials remind tourists that these aren't just "friendly birds" but also a serious threat to the city's architecture.

These laws illustrate that, while strange, many had a purpose in their time—though today they evoke more smiles and confusion than compliance. They're a testament to how creative and quirky legal history can be!

Subchapter 3: Laws Created by Accident

Some laws were enacted entirely by accident or due to a misunderstanding of the situation. Instead of being corrected, they persisted and remain in force today, puzzling both locals and visitors. Here are 10 examples of such laws:

No Fake Mustaches in Church – Alabama, USA

This law was passed in the 19th century to prevent disruptions during church services. Fake mustaches, especially comedic ones, were considered provocative and a source of laughter during sermons.

Illegal to Step on Money – Thailand

In Thailand, stepping on banknotes or coins is forbidden because they bear the image of the king. While the intent was to protect the monarch's dignity, the law is sometimes applied even when someone accidentally steps on money.

No Playing the Accordion at Night – Switzerland

Initially created to limit noise in densely populated areas, this law originated after one particularly loud accordionist disturbed the peace in the 1950s. Despite its specificity, the law remains on the books.

No Cycling with a Pot on Your Head – Germany

This law was introduced in a German city after a cyclist wore a pot as a helmet, causing both laughter and road hazards. The rule was a reaction to the absurdity of the situation but remains formally enforceable.

Law Against Dogs and Cats "Uniting" – Alaska, USA

In a small Alaskan town, a law forbids letting dogs and cats roam the streets together. It was passed accidentally when a local official misunderstood a resident's complaint about fighting animals.

No Bacon Frying in Public – Minnesota, USA

This law was enacted after a single incident where frying bacon over an open flame caused a fire. Despite being a response to a one-off event, it still technically applies today.

Ilegal to Be Too Happy – Italy

In the town of Aosta, there's a law that bans "excessive cheerfulness" at funerals. It was introduced after a group of drunk mourners caused a ruckus, leading to public complaints.

No Drinking Alcohol While Riding a Horse – Colorado, USA

This law was created after a drunken cowboy caused chaos in town, but it's still taken seriously today. It applies to situations where a horse is considered a mode of transportation.

No Wearing Crowns in Parks – Canada

In a Canadian city, a law bans wearing crowns in public parks. This odd rule stems from a 19th-century incident where a theater group performed in a park, destroying plants, and blamed it on their "royal coronation."

No Hanging Underwear in Windows – India

This law exists in some parts of India to maintain city aesthetics. It was passed accidentally when a resident misinterpreted a complaint about "illegal hanging items" as referring to underwear rather than advertising banners.

These laws demonstrate how even the most peculiar situations can shape legislation. Funny and absurd, they highlight how unpredictable lawmaking can be, with origins that are often full of surprises.

Chapter 9: Everyday Surprises

Subchapter 1: Why Are Some Objects Designed So Strangely?

Some everyday objects seem designed more to confuse than to assist, but even the strangest designs often have a purpose—albeit one that might be difficult to grasp at first glance. Here are 15 fascinating facts about oddly designed objects:

Holes in Pen Caps

Have you noticed the tiny holes in most pen caps? They're not a mistake—they're there for safety. If someone accidentally swallows the cap, the hole ensures they can still breathe.

Strangely Placed Pockets in Women's Pants

Pockets in women's pants are often smaller or oddly placed, much to the frustration of wearers. The reason? Fashion history—designers assumed women carried purses, so pockets were deemed unnecessary.

Spoon in Yogurt Containers

Some yogurt containers include a foldable spoon that's awkward to use. Its design saves space in the packaging, though using it can be a challenge.

Weirdly Bent Hairdresser's Scissors

Hairdresser's scissors have asymmetrical handles that look uncomfortable but are designed to keep the stylist's hand in an ergonomic position during prolonged use.

Square Watermelons from Japan

Japanese farmers grow square watermelons that might seem impractical, but they're engineered to fit perfectly into refrigerators and stack easily on store shelves.

Holes in the Ends of Keys

The small holes in the ends of keys are there for easy attachment to keyrings. They're also used in precision key-copying machines.

Arrow on Fuel Gauge in Cars

The fuel gauge in most cars has a small arrow pointing to the side of the vehicle where the fuel cap is located. A simple but incredibly useful detail that often goes unnoticed.

Holes in Wine Bottle Stoppers

Some wine stoppers have small holes that allow air to escape from inside the bottle, preventing the cork from popping out due to temperature changes.

Triangular Pizza Boxes

Square boxes for round pizzas may seem odd, but they're easier and cheaper to produce and assemble than circular boxes.

Blunt Table Knives

Table knives with rounded tips originated in 17th-century France when Cardinal Richelieu ordered them dulled to prevent fights during meals—a practical solution to a violent problem.

Oval Airplane Windows

Airplane windows are rounded to prevent material stress at the corners, which could lead to cracks and structural failure during flight.

Unusual Shapes of Perfume Bottles

Many perfume bottles have impractical, eye-catching shapes. These designs are meant to grab attention on store shelves and convey the uniqueness of the fragrance.

Holes in Crocs

The distinctive holes in Crocs may look decorative, but they provide ventilation and help prevent water from pooling inside the shoes.

Plastic Tips on Shoelaces

Known as aglets, these tips make it much easier to thread laces through eyelets. Without them, laces would fray and become unusable.

The Tricky USB Plug

USB plugs notoriously only fit after a few tries. Their asymmetrical design was chosen for cost-saving reasons, even though it's less user-friendly.

Each of these objects may seem strange at first glance, but their designs often have a hidden logic. They're a reminder that the mundane is full of surprises and cleverly concealed details.

Subchapter 2: Life Stories Funnier Than Fiction

Real life can be more surprising and comedic than even the best movie scripts or novels. Here are 10 extraordinary and funny life stories that sound like jokes but genuinely happened:

The Woman Who Crashed Her Own Bachelorette Party

In 2018, a Canadian woman went to a bar for a drink and accidentally stumbled upon a party—her own bachelorette party. Her friends had forgotten to inform her about the event, and she ended up arriving there for an entirely different reason.

The "Chocolate King" at the Airport

A passenger at a Turkish airport refused to pay extra fees for 7 kilograms of chocolate in excess baggage. Instead, he began eating the chocolate on the spot, sharing it with fellow passengers and airport staff. The problem was "eaten" in a matter of minutes.

The Boss Who Forgot to Fire His Employee

In the U.S., an employee learned that his termination had been scheduled for a Friday, but his boss forgot to have the conversation. The employee continued working for three more years before the oversight was noticed.

The "Lost" Student Who Simply Switched Classrooms

A British university student got lost on campus and accidentally attended a chemistry lecture instead of his psychology class. He believed it to be an introductory theory course for his major and kept attending for half a semester.

Pizza Order That Saved a Life

In the U.S., a woman trapped at home by her partner ordered pizza online and included a plea for help in the "notes" section. The pizzeria staff called the police, who rescued her—and the pizza was delivered as well.

The Stowaway Cat on a Move

A German family moved to a new apartment, only to discover two days later that their cat had been hiding in a closet the entire time. The feline traveled 200 kilometers and emerged from the closet hungry but unharmed.

The Kangaroo Hopping Through the City Streets

Residents of Dublin reported a kangaroo hopping through the city streets. It turned out the kangaroo had escaped from a private zoo and became a sensation in the city for several hours before being safely captured.

Pizza Delivered… After 10 Years

In Canada, a man received a pizza he had ordered online a decade earlier. A system glitch delayed the order for ten years. Amusingly, he ate it and said it tasted great.

Locked in a Bank Vault Overnight

A bank employee in London accidentally locked himself in a vault overnight while organizing documents. He spent the night surrounded by cash and gold bars until the vault was reopened the following morning.

A Letter Delivered 300 Years Late

In 2022, a letter intended for delivery in the 18th century was discovered in the Netherlands. Despite arriving three centuries late, its content—asking for financial assistance—was surprisingly relatable to modern times.

These stories show that life often writes the most unexpected, hilarious scripts, often far more unpredictable and entertaining than any fiction could ever be.

Subchapter 3: The Absurdities of the Modern World

The modern world is full of situations so strange and improbable that it's hard to believe they're real. Here are 10 absurdities proving that reality can be more surreal than fiction:

Virtual Potatoes Sold for Thousands of Dollars

In the NFT (Non-Fungible Token) era, a digital potato was sold for over $50,000. It's just an image of a virtual vegetable, but buyers believed it had unique collectible value.

Rent-a-Friend by the Hour

In Japan and the U.S., companies offer "friend rentals" for events, weddings, or even walks. It's a legitimate service, but it feels like something out of a futuristic TV show.

Luxury Product Vending Machines

In Dubai, vending machines dispense gold bars instead of snacks. It's no joke—customers can grab valuable metals as casually as a bag of chips.

Paid "Safe Spot" in Lines

In some cities, people offer to stand in line for a fee, so someone else can jump ahead. During the pandemic, this service became especially popular for buying game consoles or securing vaccine appointments.

"Stupidity Tax" in Sweden

Sweden introduced a tax on organizing illegal card game tournaments, which locals humorously dubbed a "stupidity tax."

Fashion for Empty "Luxury" Packaging

Luxury brands started selling empty packaging—bags, boxes, even bottles—as collectible items. The price? Hundreds of dollars for nothing but the container.

Queues for Nothing

In 1990s Russia, people would line up without knowing why. When a crowd formed, it was assumed something valuable would soon be for sale—though no one knew what it might be.

Paid Air for Tires

In some countries, gas stations began charging for tire air pumps. This led many drivers to hunt for "free air refill" stations.

Influencers Promoting Bottled Water for Thousands

Certain brands sell "luxury water" for hundreds or even thousands of dollars, claiming it comes from remote mountains or is "infused with moon energy."

Furniture with Holes as a Design Trend

Modern interior design trends celebrate furniture with holes as "functional art." For instance, tables with large gaps in the middle sell for thousands of dollars, even though their practicality is highly questionable.

These absurdities show how modern creativity often goes overboard, but also how many seemingly strange things become part of our everyday lives.

Chapter 10: Stories That Are Hard to Believe but True

Subchapter 1: Heroes from Real Life

Sometimes reality gives us heroes who seem to have stepped out of movies or comic books. Their actions, determination, and extraordinary stories make it hard to believe they truly existed. Here are 15 fascinating facts about real-life heroes:

Witold Pilecki – Volunteer for Auschwitz

Polish soldier Witold Pilecki willingly allowed himself to be arrested and sent to Auschwitz to gather intelligence. He organized a resistance movement inside the camp and escaped after two years, bringing the world the first detailed reports of the Holocaust.

Hiroo Onoda – The Soldier Who Didn't Surrender for 30 Years

Japanese soldier Hiroo Onoda hid on a Philippine island for 29 years after World War II, convinced the conflict was still ongoing. He finally surrendered when his former commander personally told him the war had ended.

Nicholas Winton – The British Schindler

Nicholas Winton saved 669 Jewish children from the Holocaust by organizing their evacuation to Britain. He kept his heroic deeds a secret for over 50 years until his wife discovered old documents detailing his actions.

Florence Nightingale – The Lady with the Lamp

During the Crimean War, Florence Nightingale revolutionized battlefield healthcare, introducing hygiene standards that saved thousands of soldiers' lives.

Stanisław Jerzy Lec – Escape from a Death Camp

Polish writer Stanisław Jerzy Lec escaped a concentration camp by hiding in a barrel of waste. After his escape, he joined the resistance and continued his literary career.

Desmond Doss – The Weaponless Hero

Desmond Doss, a medic in World War II, refused to carry a weapon but saved 75 wounded soldiers on Okinawa's battlefield. His acts of bravery earned him the Medal of Honor.

Oskar Dirlewanger – Janitor Who Saved a City

In 1958, in Japan, Oskar Dirlewanger, a janitor, saved hundreds during a fire by leading them out of a burning building.

John Rabe – The Angel of Nanking

During the Nanking Massacre, German businessman John Rabe saved thousands of Chinese citizens by creating a safety zone. He leveraged his Nazi Party connections to negotiate with Japanese forces.

Eugen Lazowski – The Doctor Who Fooled the Nazis

Polish doctor Eugen Lazowski faked a typhus epidemic to protect an entire village from Nazi raids. His clever ruse saved thousands from deportation.

Chiune Sugihara – The Japanese Diplomat Who Saved Jews

While stationed in Lithuania, Japanese diplomat Chiune Sugihara issued thousands of visas to Jewish refugees, enabling their escape from the Holocaust, defying his government's orders.

Nancy Wake – The White Mouse

Nancy Wake, one of the most wanted agents of the French Resistance during World War II, repeatedly outwitted the Gestapo with her cunning strategies.

Abdul Sattar Edhi – The Man Who Helped Everyone

Pakistani philanthropist Abdul Sattar Edhi founded a charity providing free healthcare, shelter, and education to millions. His fleet of ambulances was ready to assist anyone in need, regardless of background.

Irena Sendler – The Mother of the Warsaw Ghetto

Polish activist Irena Sendler rescued 2,500 Jewish children by smuggling them out of the Warsaw Ghetto and finding them safe homes with false identities.

Aleksei Ananenko – The Chernobyl Rescuer

During the Chernobyl disaster, Aleksei Ananenko and two colleagues volunteered to enter the flooded reactor to prevent a larger explosion. Fully aware it was a death mission, they saved millions of lives.

Aron Ralston – The Man Who Cut Off His Own Arm to Survive

In 2003, climber Aron Ralston became trapped in a canyon when a boulder pinned his arm. After five days, he amputated his own arm to free himself and survive. His ordeal was adapted into the film 127 Hours.

These stories prove that heroism isn't confined to fiction. Real people, their courage, and their extraordinary deeds inspire us and remind us that anyone can become a hero.

Subchapter 2: Accidental Events That Changed the World

Sometimes, the most significant events in human history were pure accidents. Here are 10 situations that weren't planned but had a profound impact on the world:

Penicillin – The Accidental Discovery of Antibiotics

In 1928, Alexander Fleming noticed that a mold on his petri dish killed surrounding bacteria. This led to the discovery of penicillin, the first antibiotic, which revolutionized medicine.

Columbus Discovers America While Searching for India

In 1492, Christopher Columbus set out to find a route to India but accidentally landed in the Caribbean. His voyage initiated the colonization of the Americas, reshaping world history.

The Invention of the Microwave Oven

In the 1940s, Percy Spencer was working on radar technology when he noticed a chocolate bar in his pocket melting. This serendipitous moment led to the creation of the microwave oven, a staple of modern kitchens.

The Industrial Revolution Sparked by a Faulty Engine

In 1712, Thomas Newcomen was trying to fix a coal mine pump when he inadvertently created a steam engine. This invention marked the beginning of the Industrial Revolution, transforming global manufacturing.

The Creation of Post-It Notes

In 1968, Spencer Silver was developing a strong adhesive but ended up with a weak one that could be easily removed and reused. This accidental innovation became the iconic Post-It Notes.

The Qing Dynasty Began with an Orphaned Boy

Nurhaci, who founded China's Qing Dynasty, survived a military raid that killed his family. As an adult, he established an empire that ruled China for over 300 years.

Coca-Cola – A Medicine Turned Soft Drink

In 1886, pharmacist John Stith Pemberton created a syrup to alleviate headaches. When it was accidentally mixed with carbonated water, Coca-Cola was born, becoming one of the most popular beverages worldwide.

The Fall of the Berlin Wall Due to a Communication Error

In 1989, East Germany's spokesperson, Günter Schabowski, mistakenly announced that borders were open "effective immediately" instead of at a planned date. Crowds rushed the Berlin Wall, leading to its historic fall.

Potato Chips Were Born from Annoyance

In 1853, New York chef George Crum sliced potatoes thinly and fried them out of frustration over a customer's complaints about thick fries. This mistake gave the world the beloved snack, potato chips.

The Discovery of Plutonium

In 1940, scientists conducting uranium experiments accidentally discovered a new element—plutonium. This discovery became crucial for nuclear energy and the development of atomic bombs.

These accidental breakthroughs demonstrate that sometimes a small mistake, unexpected phenomenon, or stroke of luck can shape the course of history. Life's greatest surprises often lead to the most transformative outcomes!

Subchapter 3: Urban Legends That Turned Out to Be True

Urban legends often sound like fairy tales or jokes, but sometimes they hold a kernel of truth—and in some cases, they are entirely factual. Here are 10 stories that began as myths but ultimately turned out to be real:

Alligator in New York City Sewers

For years, stories circulated about alligators living in New York City's sewers. While it seemed like a myth, a real alligator over a meter long was indeed captured in 1935, confirming some truth to the tale.

A Body Under the Hotel Bed

The chilling legend of tourists discovering a corpse hidden under a hotel mattress has been confirmed multiple times. Cases of such grim discoveries have occurred in places like the U.S. and Mexico, making this urban legend a horrifying reality.

A Stranger Living in the Attic

The idea of someone secretly living in your attic seems far-fetched, yet in 2008 in Japan, a man discovered a woman who had been living in his closet for a year, quietly using his food and space without detection.

A Tooth in a Hamburger

The story of finding a human tooth in fast food sounds implausible, but in 2014, a customer in Japan found a tooth in their hamburger at a fast-food chain, proving the legend true in this case.

Crocodiles in Lake Michigan

Tales of crocodiles lurking in Lake Michigan seemed like pure fiction until 2013, when a small crocodile was caught there. Authorities believe it was released into the wild by a pet owner.

A Ghost in the Closet

Stories of "ghosts" opening closet doors turned out to be true for one Los Angeles resident. She discovered the "ghost" was a homeless man who had entered through an open window and hidden in her closet.

Radioactive Jewelry

An urban legend claimed jewelry from the 1940s and 1950s was radioactive. This was confirmed when scientists discovered that some pieces contained uranium, made before the dangers of radiation were fully understood.

A Mind-Control Video Game: Polybius

The legend of "Polybius," a game said to induce hallucinations in the 1980s, turned out to have some basis in reality. In 2021, it was revealed that experimental arcade machines at the time could cause migraines and dizziness.

Deadly Treats with Hidden Blades

The story of needles or razors hidden in food seemed like an urban myth until 2018, when Australia faced a national scare after needles were found embedded in fruits like strawberries. It was later identified as a deliberate act of sabotage.

A Man Living in the Walls

The eerie legend of a "man in the walls" came true in 2007 in Colorado, where a homeowner discovered a man secretly living within the walls of their house, sneaking out only when the residents were away.

These stories prove that even the most bizarre urban legends can sometimes hold truth. Life can indeed be stranger than fiction—and in the most unexpected ways!

Chapter 11: Conclusion

The world is full of surprises—strange, amusing, and fascinating facts that often sound like fiction but are undeniably true. Throughout the eleven chapters of this book, we've explored the mysteries of animals, humans, space, technology, law, and everyday life, proving that reality can be far more extraordinary than we ever imagined.

Let's revisit some of the unforgettable highlights that are sure to stay with you:

- Penguins give each other pebbles as love tokens—a gesture that's both romantic and practical, as the stones are used to build nests.

- Ketchup was once a medicine—marketed as a remedy for indigestion and sold in pill form.

- Martian sand dunes can "sing"—vibrations caused by shifting sand produce sounds reminiscent of low musical tones.

- Fake mustaches were banned in Alabama churches—to prevent distractions during worship services.

- Microwaves were invented by accident—it all started with chocolate melting in a scientist's pocket.

- Alligators in New York City sewers—long considered an urban legend until one was actually captured there.

- The Sun accounts for 99.86% of the Solar System's mass—and rest?

That's everything else: planets, moons, and asteroids.

- A robot vacuum "attacked" its owner—accidentally sucking up their hair while they were asleep.

- Potato chips were invented out of frustration—a chef created them to teach a lesson to a complaining customer.

- A woman secretly lived in someone's closet for a year—proving that reality can sometimes mirror the strangest urban legends.

Each story, fact, and absurdity we've uncovered demonstrates just how diverse and surprising the world can be. From pebble-gifting penguins to people accidentally altering history, this kaleidoscope of knowledge reminds us to approach life with curiosity and a sense of humor.

Final Thoughts

We hope this book not only informed but also entertained and inspired you. The world is brimming with bizarre facts, and now you're a collector of these delightful oddities. Who knows? One day, you might create your own list of things that seem too strange to be true- but absolutely are. ☺

Thank you for joining us on this journey through extraordinary stories!